BIO
921
WILDER

Greene, Carol

Laura Ingalls Wilder

$14.60

BIO
921
WILDER

Greene, Carol

Laura Ingalls
Wilder

$14.60

DATE	BORROWER'S NAME	

© THE BAKER & TAYLOR CO.

A ROOKIE BIOGRAPHY

LAURA INGALLS WILDER

Author of the Little House Books

By Carol Greene

CHILDRENS PRESS ®

CHICAGO

This book is for Pat Taylor.

Laura Ingalls Wilder

LIBRARY OF CONGRESS
Library of Congress Cataloging-in-Publication Data

Greene, Carol.
    Laura Ingalls Wilder : author of the Little house books / by Carol
Greene
        p.   cm. — (A Rookie biography)
    Summary: A biography of Laura Ingalls Wilder, who actually lived in
the little houses about which she wrote.
    ISBN 0-516-04212-2
    1. Wilder, Laura Ingalls, 1867-1957—Biography—Juvenile literature.
2. Authors, American—20th century—Biography—Juvenile literature.
3. Children's stories—Authorship—Juvenile literature. 4. Frontier and
pioneer life—Juvenile literature. [1. Wilder, Laura Ingalls, 1867-1957.
2. Authors, American.] I. Title. II. Series: Greene, Carol. Rookie
biography.
PS3545.I342Z66   1990
813'.52—dc20
[B]
[92]   89-25362
                                                   CIP
                                                   AC

Laura Ingalls Wilder
was a real person.
She lived from 1867 to 1957.
Her life was
full of stories.
She told some of them
in her books.
This is her story too.

TABLE OF CONTENTS

In 1978, a copy of the cabin that Laura Ingalls wrote about
in *The Little House in the Big Woods* was built near Pepin, Wisconsin.

Chapter 1

Little Houses

Laura Ingalls was born in a little house in the big Wisconsin woods. Soon her family moved to a little house in Missouri.

A copy of the cabin that Laura wrote about
in *Little House on the Prairie* stands outside
Independence, Kansas.

Laura was too small
to remember that house.
But she did remember
the little house
on the Kansas prairie.

There a neighbor swam
across a stormy creek
to bring the Ingalls children
their Christmas gifts.

Carrie, Mary, and Laura Ingalls

Each girl got
a penny,
a tin cup,
a little cake,
and a stick
of candy.
They were too
happy to speak.
Laura never
forgot that
kind neighbor.

In Kansas, she saw Indians.
She heard their war cries.
One day, she watched them
leave their homeland forever.

Soon the Ingalls family left too.
They went back
to the big Wisconsin woods.
Laura liked to travel.
She liked to look out
the back of the wagon.

Everybody that Laura loved
traveled with her.
There were Pa and Ma,
sister Mary and baby Carrie.
There was the good dog, Jack.

Last, there was Pa's fiddle.
Many nights that fiddle
sang Laura to sleep.
It made her feel at home
wherever she was.

Charles "Pa" and Caroline "Ma" Ingalls

Pa's fiddle

Back in the big woods,
Laura went to school.
She played with cousins.
She helped Ma and Pa.
When snow fell, she stayed
warm in the little house.

But when Laura was seven,
Pa wanted to move again.
This time the family went
to Walnut Grove, Minnesota.

There Laura
found a door in
the side of a hill.
Behind the door lay
her dugout home
on the banks
of Plum Creek.

**Plum Creek near
Walnut Grove, Minnesota**

Laura went to a one-room schoolhouse.

After a while,
Pa built a real house.
Then Laura went to school.
She met new friends.
She met stuck-up
Nellie Owens too.

Pa wanted to raise crops.
He worked hard on his land.
But clouds of grasshoppers
ate all the crops.

At last, Pa gave up.
He loaded the wagon,
and the Ingalls family
moved on again.

Chapter 2

The Road to Dakota

First the wagon rolled east
to Uncle Peter's farm.
There Laura had a job.
She brought the cows
home from pasture each day.

Laura loved the farm.
She picked flowers, waded,
and watched the squirrels.
Sometimes she forgot the cows.
Then they brought *her* home.

The Masters Hotel in Burr Oak, Iowa, today (left)
and how it looked when Pa worked there (right)

Soon the Ingalls family moved
to Burr Oak, Iowa.
Pa helped run a hotel.
Laura and Mary went to school.
One spring day,
baby Grace was born.

Laura was happy in Burr Oak.
But Pa wasn't.
He couldn't earn enough money.
He missed the open spaces.
So he moved his family
back to Walnut Grove.

There Mary became very sick.
After that sickness,
Mary couldn't see anymore.
She was blind.

Pa told Laura
she must see *for* Mary.
So Laura learned to put
the things she saw into words.
Then Mary could
see them in her mind.

Silver Lake (above) and the
Ingalls family house (left)
in De Smet, South Dakota.

One day, Pa went west again.
He worked for the railroad.
Ma and the girls followed him
to the shores of Silver Lake
in Dakota Territory.

The Ingalls family:
Ma, Carrie, Laura,
Pa, Grace, Mary

Pa built the
kitchen cupboard
and the dresser
pictured below.

Life wasn't easy there.
Pa did many jobs.
Sometimes the Ingalls family
lived by the lake.
Sometimes they lived
in the prairie town of De Smet.

Lake Henry
in the Dakota
Territory

Summers could be very hot.
Winters could be very cold.
One long winter,
blizzards cut De Smet off
from the rest of the world.
People almost starved.

But Laura loved Dakota Territory.
She went to school
when she could.
She took a sewing job too.

Laura and Carrie once went to school in this building (left).
Pa built this house in De Smet in 1887.

She wanted to help send Mary
to a school in Iowa,
a school for blind people.
At last, Mary went.

Laura was glad that
her sister could go on learning.
But she missed Mary.
From now on, the family
would not be the same.

Chapter 3

Growing Up

When Laura was 15,
she went to work.
For a while, she taught
in a tiny prairie school.
She lived with strangers.
That was hard.

Each weekend,
Almanzo Wilder
took her home
in his sleigh.
He was ten years older.
Laura liked him.
But she thought
he was just a friend.

Almanzo James Wilder

Then Laura stopped teaching
and went back to school.
But soon she had more jobs.
She kept seeing Almanzo too.

When Laura was 17, Almanzo
asked her to marry him.
She said yes.
A year later, they got married
and moved to their own
little house on the prairie.

Laura and Almanzo Wilder shortly after their marriage

Almanzo loved farming.
But it was a hard life.
The new family was poor.
Soon they had a baby girl.
Laura called her Rose.

Rose was two years and
four months old when
this picture was taken.

Laura had to face many troubles.

Then came some bad years.
First the barn burned down.
Next, Laura and Almanzo
became very sick.
After the sickness,
Almanzo couldn't walk well.

The year after that,
their new baby boy died.
Then their house burned down.

At last, they left their farm.
They moved to Minnesota.
Then they moved to Florida.
Then they came back to De Smet.
No place was right for them.

So they worked and saved.
Laura sewed and Almanzo
did many different jobs.
When they had enough money,
they loaded their wagon
and set off again.

This time Rose sat in back.
It was a long, hot trip.
But Laura and Almanzo
felt full of hope.
They knew the right place now
and they were on their way.

Laura at the spring branch on Rocky Ridge Farm (left); Almanzo posing beside an apple tree in the orchard (below)

Chapter 4

Rocky Ridge Farm

One day, the Wilder wagon
rolled into the Ozark Mountains.
Winters there were mild.
Cool breezes blew in summer.
The Wilder family found a farm
outside Mansfield, Missouri.

There were plenty of trees
and water and rocks.
"Too many rocks," thought Almanzo.
It would take hard work
to clear the land for crops.

Almanzo with his horse and buggy by the little log house

But Laura knew
it was the perfect place.
It even had apple trees!
And hard work didn't scare her.

So they bought the farm.
Laura called it
Rocky Ridge Farm.
At first, they lived
in a little log house.
Laura felt right at home.

Then they built a barn
and cleared land.
Corn, wheat, and oats grew.
Strawberries and grapes
got fat and ripe.
Apples hung from the trees.

They also raised animals—
hogs, sheep, cows, and goats.
Laura was good with hens too.

The happy years flew by.

A big new house took
the place of the log house.
Rose grew up and
became a famous writer.

The Wilder house on Rocky Ridge Farm in Mansfield, Missouri

Laura was a
busy woman.
She began
writing her
"Little House" series
in 1932.

Laura wrote articles
about farm life.
She helped start clubs
for farm women.
She started a library too.
She helped farmers get loans.

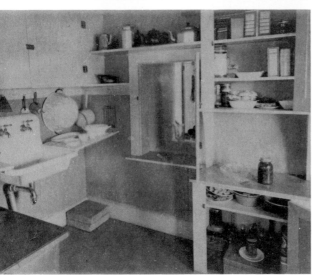

The parlor at Rocky Ridge (top), and two views of the farm kitchen Laura designed. Almanzo did all the woodwork including the kitchen cabinets.

Then one day,
when Laura was 63,
she got a letter from Rose.
Rose had an idea,
a *splendid* idea.

Laura wrote her books at this desk.
Sometimes she would wake up in the middle
of the night and write for hours.

Chapter 5

The Books

Rose wanted her mother
to write down stories
about the days when
Laura was a little girl.

Laura liked the idea.
She often thought
about those days.
So she began to write.

In her mind, she was back
with Pa, Ma, and her sisters.
The wind blew outside
their snug little house.
And Pa's fiddle sang.

Laura changed some things
to make the stories better.
But mostly she wrote
just what happened.

Rose gave the stories
to an editor in New York.
Soon they became a book,
Little House in the Big Woods.

Children loved the books that Laura wrote.

Laura thought that
her work was done.
But she was wrong.
Children loved the book.
They wrote to her
and begged for more.

So Laura wrote *Farmer Boy*.
It told Almanzo's story.
Then she wrote
Little House on the Prairie
and *On the Banks of Plum Creek*.

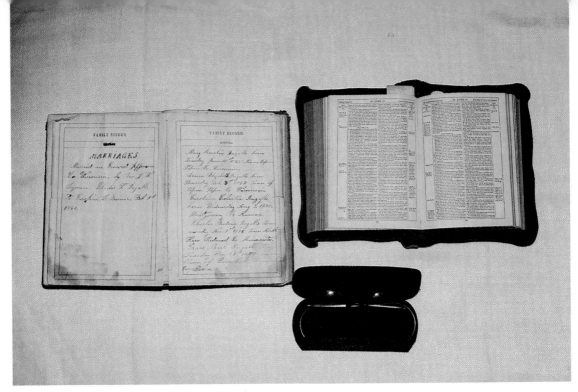

The Ingalls family Bible (left), Laura's Bible (right), and Laura's glasses

By the Shores of Silver Lake
and *The Long Winter* came next.
Children wanted still more.

Little Town on the Prairie
and *These Happy Golden Years*
were the last two books
about Laura's childhood.
Laura was 76
when they came out.

Almanzo and Laura in 1942

Six years later, Almanzo died.
He was 92.
Laura lived on
at Rocky Ridge Farm
for eight more years.
She died when she was 90.

Laura's books won awards (above left). Visitors to
Rocky Ridge Farm can see her awards and bookcase (right).

Laura wrote this letter to her young readers
and in it she talked about the values she thought were
the most important in living a good life.

The Little House books are stories of long ago. The way we live and your schools
are much different now, so many changes have made living and learning easier.
But the real things haven't changed. It is still best to be honest and truthful; to make
the most of what we have; to be happy with simple pleasures and to be cheerful and
have courage when things go wrong.

With love to you all and best wishes for your happiness, I am,

*Yours sincerely
Laura Ingalls Wilder*

Over the years, she got
many letters from children.
She answered as many
letters as she could.

In one letter, she said,
"Remember, it is not the things
you have that make you happy.
It is love and kindness
and helping each other
and just plain being good."

Laura Ingalls Wilder
believed that.
It was the secret
of all her little houses.

Important Dates

1867 February 7—Born at Pepin, Wisconsin, to
      Charles and Caroline Ingalls

1869 Moved to Kansas

1871 Moved back to Pepin, Wisconsin

1874 Moved to Walnut Grove, Minnesota

1879 Moved to De Smet, Dakota Territory

1885 Married Almanzo Wilder

1886 Daughter Rose born

1894 Moved to Rocky Ridge Farm near Mansfield,
      Missouri

1932 *Little House in the Big Woods* published

1957 February 10—Died at Rocky Ridge Farm

Books by Laura Ingalls Wilder

Little House in the Big Woods
Farmer Boy
Little House on the Prairie
On the Banks of Plum Creek
By the Shores of Silver Lake
The Long Winter
Little Town on the Prairie
These Happy Golden Years
*The First Four Years**
*On the Way Home**
*West from Home**

* These three books tell about Laura's life as a grown-up.

All of these books are published by Harper & Row, Publishers, Inc., New York.

INDEX

Page numbers in boldface type indicate illustrations.

PHOTO CREDITS

ABOUT THE AUTHOR

Carol Greene has degrees in English literature and musicology. She has worked in international exchange programs, as an editor, and as a teacher. She now lives in St. Louis, Missouri, and writes full-time. She has published more than eighty books. Others in the Rookie Biographies series include *Benjamin Franklin, Pocahontas, Martin Luther King, Jr., Christopher Columbus, Abraham Lincoln, Beatrix Potter, Robert E. Lee, Ludwig van Beethoven, Jackie Robinson, Jacques Cousteau,* and *Daniel Boone.*